A SHAKESPEARE TREASURY

52 Great Shakespearean Speeches
A Year with William Shakespeare Week by Week

Edited by Kate Emery Pogue

ISBN: 978-1-64314-220-3 (Hardback)

AuthorsPress
California, USA
www.authorspress.com

Operas for Adults
The Impresario
Hadleyberg
The Mask of Evil

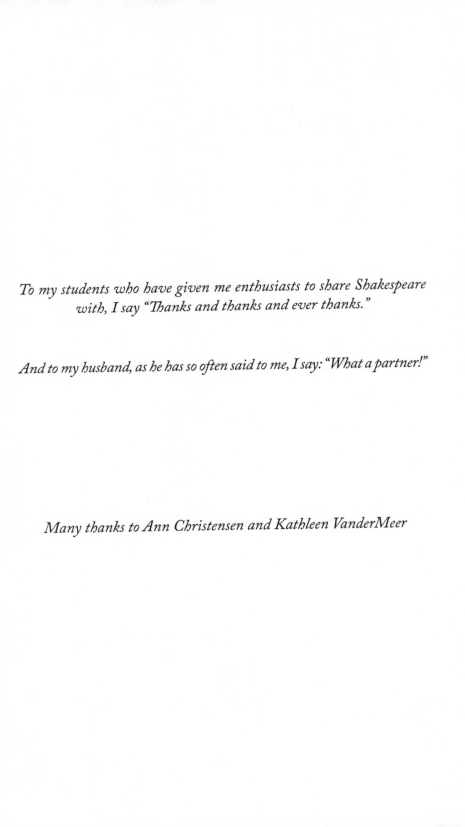

To my students who have given me enthusiasts to share Shakespeare with, I say "Thanks and thanks and ever thanks."

And to my husband, as he has so often said to me, I say: "What a partner!"

Many thanks to Ann Christensen and Kathleen VanderMeer

A YEAR WITH WILLIAM SHAKESPEARE

52 GREAT SHAKESPEAREAN SPEECHES

Table of Contents

30.	Julius Caesar	Act III Scene 2	Brutus
31.	Julius Caesar	Act III Scene 2	Mark Antony
32.	As You Like It	Act II Scene 7	Jacques
33.	Twelfth Night	Act II Scene 1	Viola

Great Tragedies and Problem Plays

34.	Hamlet	Act I Scene 2	Hamlet
35.	Hamlet	Act II Scene 2	Hamlet
36.	Hamlet	Act III Scene 1	Hamlet
37.	Hamlet	Act III Scene 2	Hamlet
38.	Hamlet	Act IV Scene 4	Hamlet
39.	Hamlet	Act IV Scene 7	Gertrude
40.	Troilus and Cressida	Act III Scene 3	Ulysses
41.	King Lear	Act I Scene 2	Edmund
42.	King Lear	Act II Scene 2	Kent
43.	Othello	Act IV Scene 3	Emilia
44.	Othello	Act V Scene 2	Othello
45.	Measure for Measure	Act III Scene 1	Claudio
46.	Macbeth	Act III Scene 2	Macbeth
47.	Macbeth	Act V Scene 4	Macbeth
48.	Antony and Cleopatra	Act V Scene 2	Cleopatra

The Late Romances

49.	The Winter's Tale	Act IV Scene 4	Perdita
50.	The Tempest	Act III Scene 3	Caliban
51.	The Tempest	Act IV Scene 1	Prospero
52.	The Tempest	Act V Scene 1	Prospero

A SHAKESPEARE TREASURY

A Year with William Shakespeare Week by Week

INTRODUCTION

This book is made up of fifty-two great Shakespearean speeches. Long and short, spoken by male and female characters, in prose and in verse, they have been chosen to give you, the reader, the joy of exploring in a single volume a wide variety of Shakespeare's best writing.

Reading the full script of a Shakespeare play can be intimidating. The language is difficult. It's sometimes hard to figure out what is happening. The characters are unfamiliar. But I hope the selections here can begin to give you a sense of why people for over four hundred years have loved Shakespeare, why students have gathered, as mine have for four decades, to read and discuss his work.

Some considerations as you open this book:

The speeches are arranged (as much as can be determined) in the order in which they were written i.e. during the quarter century between 1588 and 1613.

All were written to be acted, so try reading them out loud and see how that opens up your understanding of the text.

Look for the writing, even in the early plays, to be rich and complex. Shakespeare was taught from the time he was young to use figures of speech. He relished *simile* and *metaphor* (for instance, Romeo calls Juliet "a rich jewel in an Ethiope's ear" (p. 18), Jaques tells us the world is a stage (p. 53) while Macbeth calls life a "brief candle" (p. 74) and John of Gaunt calls England "This other-Eden, demi-paradise" (p. 21). Note selection #1 in this book for Shakespeare's use of *anaphora*, (the repetition of a word at the beginning of a sequence of phrases) or selection #3 for the use of *systrophe* (the piling up of descriptive words). He loved *personification* (see Richard III talking of "Grim-visaged war" (p. 4) or Constance telling us how "Grief fills the room up of my absent child, lies in his bed, walks Up and down with me." (p. 29).

Another consideration: speeches fall roughly into two categories, monologues and soliloquies. Identifying each is interesting because Shakespeare used them differently. The word "monologue" comes from *mono* meaning one and *logos*, the Latin for word. They are speeches given by one individual to another character or group of characters. They are most often energetic and rhetorical, used to stimulate, spur, enliven, or to move to action. Henry V's thrilling Crispin's Day speech (p. 43) or Mark Antony's "Friends, Romans, countrymen," (p. 48) are inspired monologues of this kind. The character is speaking to an on-stage audience.

But in a soliloquy (coming from *solo* or *solus*) a character is by himself on stage and we are invited into the workings of his mind: most of Hamlet's speeches, notably "To be or not to be" (p. 57) are soliloquies.

Monologues always involve other characters and play out in scenes and relationships. But there are legitimate questions about how soliloquies should be performed nowadays. From the middle of the 19th century nearly to the present day, realism reigned in the theatre. Characters had to act as people do in "real life;" they had to be "believable." A person talking to himself or a character talking to the audience was not tolerated because it was not "believable."

In the theatre, as in the rest of life, technology drives change and technology has impacted the performance of Shakespeare's great speeches. From the beginning of the twentieth century to the present day, stage lighting and film close-ups have had the power to focus the attention of the audience on the actor's face, most evocatively on his eyes. This technique has encouraged actors and directors to assume that the character soliloquizing is speaking to himself. Examples are found in Laurence Olivier's and Kenneth Branagh's films of **Hamlet**, for instance, where they choose to speak some (though not all) the famous soliloquies in voice-over: the character, his face still, in effect listens to his own thoughts which are heard spoken in the background.

But recently scholars have argued that an Elizabethan actor/character speaking a soliloquy was not in fact speaking to himself. He was, surprising to us, most likely directly engaging the audience. This realization came in part from a revaluing of the influence that the story-telling theatre of the middle ages had on the Elizabethan theater. Following medieval convention, and not having the power to control focus with changing light, Shakespeare would expect his characters speaking soliloquies to control focus and compel interest by making eye contact with members of the audience, to include them (us) in the characters' anguish and insecurities, and to make us complicit in the characters' arguments and actions. Soliloquies can thus form a bond between the character and the off-stage audience, even when that bond makes us uncomfortable, as when a villain like Richard III draws us into his machinations and direful actions.

Acknowledging Shakespeare's stage tradition (now over four hundred years old), studying the presentational style of the 17th and 18th centuries, then observing the modern tradition of realism, directors have to decide with each production what style of presentation will make the soliloquies of Shakespeare most effective in today's theatre.

One thing more is crucial. Consider what is happening to a character the moment he or she speaks. To better understand each monologue in this collection, I provide some context, noting whether we are dealing with a monologue or a soliloquy, where the character is, what difficulty challenges him or her, and whom the character is addressing.

For soliloquies I suggest that the audience, the listener, the reader is the person to whom the character speaks, that we are the direct recipient of the character's thoughts: actor and audience are interlocutors. We, like the audience members in Shakespeare's day, are in the characters' minds and through them, in Shakespeare's mind.

The age of the computer has opened worlds to the readers of the speeches collected here.

By typing the first line of any of these speeches into a search engine, the reader will discover analyses, commentaries, and histories to help understand the situations, the relationships, and the language that otherwise might defeat us. Even more exciting, by accessing resources like YouTube the reader will find interpretations ranging from college and high school productions to performances by some of the world's greatest actors.

Shakespeare holds a critical place in our history and culture. To know his characters is to learn about ourselves. To untangle the language of Shakespeare's monologues is to reveal breathtaking depths of meaning encoded in his extraordinary metaphors, similes and other figures of speech. Never has there been so much help in understanding, or so much reward in comprehending, the treasure that is Shakespeare. I hope that this book leads you to these discoveries week by week all year.

1.

Henry VI Part 3

Act II Scene 5 Line 1
*Henry VI, a saintly man and a reluctant king, finds himself alone on the battlefield. He meditates on his life, comparing his destiny to the life of a simple shepherd. Shakespeare will revisit the theme of the cost of being a monarch in **Henry IV** and **Henry V**. Queen Elizabeth I and King James I both requested performances of Shakespeare's history plays at court. They undoubtedly found his psychology of kings insightful and true. Note the effective rhythmic use of anaphora (starting a sequence of lines with the same word or phrase).*

King Henry

O God! me thinks it were a happy life,
To be no better than a homely swain;
To sit upon a hill, as I do now,
To carve out dials quaintly, point by point,
Thereby to see the minutes how they run,
How many make the hour full complete;
How many hours bring about the day;
How many days will finish up the year;
How many years a mortal man may live.
When this is known, then to divide the times:
So many hours must I tend my flock;
So many hours must I take my rest;
So many hours must I contemplate;
So many hours must I sport myself;
So many days my ewes have been with young;

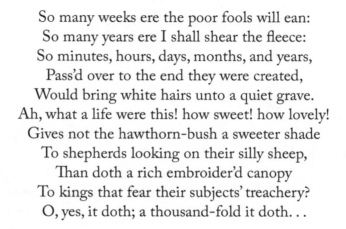

So many weeks ere the poor fools will ean:
So many years ere I shall shear the fleece:
So minutes, hours, days, months, and years,
Pass'd over to the end they were created,
Would bring white hairs unto a quiet grave.
Ah, what a life were this! how sweet! how lovely!
Gives not the hawthorn-bush a sweeter shade
To shepherds looking on their silly sheep,
Than doth a rich embroider'd canopy
To kings that fear their subjects' treachery?
O, yes, it doth; a thousand-fold it doth...

2.

Richard III

Act I Scene 1 Line 1

*This famous opening to **Richard III** shows Shakespeare's genius for ironic writing. Richard ruthlessly analyses himself, and glories in his fixation on becoming king no matter what the cost. Richard speaks directly to the audience and by sharing his plans makes us complicit in Richard's wickedness. Shakespeare knew the works of Sir Thomas More who wrote of Richard III's evil nature. But this interpretation of history has been challenged by scholars of the 20th century and the idea of a good King Richard III was popularized by Josephine Tey's book **The Daughter of Time**. There is a Ricardian Society for those seeking to rehabilitate Richard's reputation. But Richard's rival, Richmond, the first Tudor, became Henry VII on Richard's death and was a direct ancestor to Elizabeth I. Therefore, the history of the time favored a bad Richard and a good Richmond, validating Elizabeth's lineage. And certainly, Shakespeare seems to have been inspired as he explored the nature of a quintessential villain.*

Enter RICHARD Duke of GLOUCESTER, solus

Gloucester

Now is the winter of our discontent
Made glorious summer by this sun of York;
And all the clouds that lour'd upon our house
In the deep bosom of the ocean buried.
Now are our brows bound with victorious wreaths;
Our bruised arms hung up for monuments;
Our stern alarums changed to merry meetings,
Our dreadful marches to delightful measures.
Grim-visaged war hath smooth'd his wrinkled front;

And now, instead of mounting barbed steeds
To fright the souls of fearful adversaries,
He capers nimbly in a lady's chamber
To the lascivious pleasing of a lute.
But I, that am not shaped for sportive tricks,
Nor made to court an amorous looking-glass;
I, that am rudely stamp'd, and want love's majesty
To strut before a wanton ambling nymph;
I, that am curtail'd of this fair proportion,
Cheated of feature by dissembling nature,
Deformed, unfinish'd, sent before my time
Into this breathing world, scarce half made up,
And that so lamely and unfashionable
That dogs bark at me as I halt by them;
Why, I, in this weak piping time of peace,
Have no delight to pass away the time,
Unless to spy my shadow in the sun
And descant on mine own deformity:
And therefore, since I cannot prove a lover,
To entertain these fair well-spoken days,
I am determined to prove a villain
And hate the idle pleasures of these days.
Plots have I laid, inductions dangerous,
By drunken prophecies, libels and dreams,
To set my brother Clarence and the king
In deadly hate the one against the other:
And if King Edward be as true and just
As I am subtle, false and treacherous,
This day should Clarence closely be mew'd up,
About a prophecy, which says that 'G'
Of Edward's heirs the murderer shall be.
Dive, thoughts, down to my soul: here
Clarence comes.

3.

Richard III

Act I Scene 4 Line 2

*Clarence is one of the brothers of Richard, Duke of Gloucester, who must be killed if Richard is to become king. Pretending to help Clarence, Richard secretly arranges for his arrest and murder. Imprisoned, Clarence tells the jailer of a horrifying dream foreshadowing his death. Compare the scene in **Measure for Measure** (p.88) where Claudio describes his terror of death. Clarence's struggle with guilt at the end of this speech distinguish him from Richard's wickedness, though Richard, too, at the end of the play, is finally wracked with guilt.*

Clarence

O, I have pass'd a miserable night,
So full of ugly sights, of ghastly dreams,
That, as I am a Christian faithful man,
I would not spend another such a night,
Though 'twere to buy a world of happy days,
So full of dismal terror was the time! . . .
Methought that I had broken from the Tower,
And was embark'd to cross to Burgundy;
And, in my company, my brother Gloucester;
Who from my cabin tempted me to walk
Upon the hatches: thence we looked toward England,
And cited up a thousand fearful times,
During the wars of York and Lancaster
That had befall'n us. As we paced along
Upon the giddy footing of the hatches,
Me thought that Gloucester stumbled; and, in falling,
Struck me, that thought to stay him, overboard,
Into the tumbling billows of the main.

Lord, Lord! methought, what pain it was to drown!
What dreadful noise of waters in mine ears!
What ugly sights of death within mine eyes!
Methought I saw a thousand fearful wrecks;
Ten thousand men that fishes gnaw'd upon;
Wedges of gold, great anchors, heaps of pearl,
Inestimable stones, unvalued jewels,
All scatter'd in the bottom of the sea:
Some lay in dead men's skulls; and, in those holes
Where eyes did once inhabit, there were crept,
As 'twere in scorn of eyes, reflecting gems,
Which woo'd the slimy bottom of the deep,
And mock'd the dead bones that lay scatter'd by...
Often did I strive
To yield the ghost: but still the envious flood
Kept in my soul, and would not let it forth
To seek the empty, vast and wandering air;
But smother'd it within my panting bulk,
Which almost burst to belch it in the sea...
O, then began the tempest to my soul,
Who pass'd, methought, the melancholy flood,
With that grim ferryman which poets write of,
Unto the kingdom of perpetual night.
The first that there did greet my stranger soul,
Was my great father-in-law, renowned Warwick;
Who cried aloud, 'What scourge for perjury
Can this dark monarchy afford false Clarence?'
And so he vanish'd: then came wandering by
A shadow like an angel, with bright hair
Dabbled in blood; and he squeak'd out aloud,
'Clarence is come; false, fleeting, perjured Clarence,
That stabb'd me in the field by Tewksbury;
Seize on him, Furies, take him to your torments!'
With that, methought, a legion of foul fiends

Environ'd me about, and howled in mine ears
Such hideous cries, that with the very noise
I trembling waked, and for a season after
Could not believe but that I was in hell,
Such terrible impression made the dream...
O Brakenbury, I have done those things,
Which now bear evidence against my soul,
For Edward's sake; and see how he requites me!
O God! if my deep prayers cannot appease thee,
But thou wilt be avenged on my misdeeds,
Yet execute thy wrath in me alone,
O, spare my guiltless wife and my poor children!
I pray thee, gentle keeper, stay by me;
My soul is heavy, and I fain would sleep.

4.

Richard III

Act IV Scene 4 Line 61
*Queen Elizabeth (Richard's sister-in-law), the Duchess of York (Richard's mother), Lady Anne (Richard's wife) and Queen Margaret (widow of Henry VI) gather to compare their suffering at the hands of Richard, who has decimated their families. Margaret enumerates the men these women loved whom Richard has killed. That so many of them are named Edward enables Shakespeare to play rhythmically on the repetition of that name. The last eight lines of the speech build to a passionate climax. Margaret is the only character to develop over all four plays of Shakespeare's first historical tetralogy (**Henry VI Parts 1, 2** and **3** and **Richard III**), making her one of Shakespeare's most interesting female characters.*

Margaret

Bear with me; I am hungry for revenge,
And now I cloy me with beholding it.
Thy Edward he is dead, that stabb'd my Edward:
Thy other Edward dead, to quit my Edward;
Young York he is but boot, because both they
Match not the high perfection of my loss:
Thy Clarence he is dead that kill'd my Edward;
And the beholders of this tragic play,
The adulterate Hastings, Rivers, Vaughan, Grey,
Untimely smother'd in their dusky graves.
Richard yet lives, hell's black intelligencer,
Only reserved their factor, to buy souls
And send them thither: but at hand, at hand,
Ensues his piteous and unpitied end:
Earth gapes, hell burns, fiends roar, saints pray.

To have him suddenly convey'd away.
Cancel his bond of life, dear God, I pray,
That I may live to say, the dog is dead!

5.

Taming of the Shrew

Act I Scene 2 Line 197

A young man, Petruchio, comes to Padua to find a wealthy wife. His friend, Hortensio, claims to know a candidate but warns Petruchio that she is "intolerably curst and shrewd and forward." Shakespeare combines two figures of speech, rhetorical question and systrophe (the piling up of images) to express Petruchio's confidence and to set the conflict between Katharine and Petruchio that structures this ever-popular comedy.

Petruchio

Think you a little din can daunt mine ears?
Have I not in my time heard lions roar?
Have I not heard the sea puff'd up with winds
Rage like an angry boar chafed with sweat?
Have I not heard great ordnance in the field,
And heaven's artillery thunder in the skies?
Have I not in a pitched battle heard
Loud 'larums, neighing steeds, and trumpets' clang?
And do you tell me of a woman's tongue,
That gives not half so great a blow to hear
As will a chestnut in a farmer's fire?
Tush, tush! fear boys with bugs.

6.

Taming of the Shrew

Act V Scene 2 Line 135
*At the end of the play Petruchio has "tamed" Katharina by gaining
her love. He asks her to tell her newly married sister and his friend
Hortensio's bride how they should behave and especially how they
should treat their husbands. This is the first time Katharina is able
to express her love for her husband and she uses the moment to show
her gratitude for his love. The line "vail your stomachs for it is no
boot" means control or diminish your anger, for it will not help you.
Petruchio's response to this wise advice is to praise her: "Why there's a
wench. Come, kiss me, Kate."*

Katharina

Fie, fie! unknit that threatening unkind brow,
And dart not scornful glances from those eyes,
To wound thy lord, thy king, thy governor:
It blots thy beauty as frosts do bite the meads,
Confounds thy fame as whirlwinds shake fair buds,
And in no sense is meet or amiable.
A woman moved is like a fountain troubled,
Muddy, ill-seeming, thick, bereft of beauty;
And while it is so, none so dry or thirsty
Will deign to sip or touch one drop of it.
Thy husband is thy lord, thy life, thy keeper,
Thy head, thy sovereign; one that cares for thee,
And for thy maintenance commits his body
To painful labour both by sea and land,
To watch the night in storms, the day in cold,
Whilst thou liest warm at home, secure and safe;
And craves no other tribute at thy hands

But love, fair looks and true obedience;
Too little payment for so great a debt.
Such duty as the subject owes the prince
Even such a woman oweth to her husband;
And when she is froward, peevish, sullen, sour,
And not obedient to his honest will,
What is she but a foul contending rebel
And graceless traitor to her loving lord?
I am ashamed that women are so simple
To offer war where they should kneel for peace;
Or seek for rule, supremacy and sway,
When they are bound to serve, love and obey.
Why are our bodies soft and weak and smooth,
Unapt to toil and trouble in the world,
But that our soft conditions and our hearts
Should well agree with our external parts?
Come, come, you froward and unable worms!
My mind hath been as big as one of yours,
My heart as great, my reason haply more,
To bandy word for word and frown for frown;
But now I see our lances are but straws,
Our strength as weak, our weakness past compare,
That seeming to be most which we indeed least are.
Then vail your stomachs, for it is no boot,
And place your hands below your husband's foot:
In token of which duty, if he please,
My hand is ready; may it do him ease.

7.

Love's Labour's Lost

Act IV Scene 3 Line 316

*In the beginning of **Love's Labour's Lost** four young aristocratic men (one of them the King of Navarre) take a vow to spend three years in study, removed from the world and especially sequestered from women. A state visit from the Princess of France interrupts their plan as the men instantly fall in love with the Princess and her ladies. Berowne is the one lord who objects to the idea of staying cloistered for three years and takes this moment toward the end of the play to tell his friends that love for women is not a distraction from learning but will lead them to what is most important to be learned in life. Of all fifty-two of the speeches collected here I think this is my favorite.*

BEROWNE

O, we have made a vow to study, lords,
And in that vow we have forsworn our books.
For when would you, my liege, or you, or you,
In leaden contemplation have found out
Such fiery numbers as the prompting eyes
Of beauty's tutors have enrich'd you with?
Other slow arts entirely keep the brain;
And therefore, finding barren practisers,
Scarce show a harvest of their heavy toil:
But love, first learned in a lady's eyes,
Lives not alone immured in the brain;
But, with the motion of all elements,
Courses as swift as thought in every power,
And gives to every power a double power,
Above their functions and their offices.
It adds a precious seeing to the eye;

A lover's eyes will gaze an eagle blind;
A lover's ear will hear the lowest sound,
When the suspicious head of theft is stopp'd:
Love's feeling is more soft and sensible
Than are the tender horns of cockl'd snails;
Love's tongue proves dainty Bacchus gross in taste:
For valour, is not Love a Hercules,
Still climbing trees in the Hesperides?
Subtle as Sphinx; as sweet and musical
As bright Apollo's lute, strung with his hair:
And when Love speaks, the voice of all the gods
Makes heaven drowsy with the harmony.
Never durst poet touch a pen to write
Until his ink were temper'd with Love's sighs;
O, then his lines would ravish savage ears
And plant in tyrants mild humility.
From women's eyes this doctrine I derive:
They sparkle still the right Promethean fire;
They are the books, the arts, the academes,
That show, contain and nourish all the world:
Else none at all in ought proves excellent.
Then fools you were these women to forswear,
Or keeping what is sworn, you will prove fools.
For wisdom's sake, a word that all men love,
Or for love's sake, a word that loves all men,
Or for men's sake, the authors of these women,
Or women's sake, by whom we men are men,
Let us once lose our oaths to find ourselves,
Or else we lose ourselves to keep our oaths.
It is religion to be thus forsworn,
For charity itself fulfills the law,
And who can sever love from charity?

8.

Romeo and Juliet

Act I Scene 3 line 16
*Unique among Shakespeare's plays, **Romeo and Juliet** is a comedy for the first half and a tragedy in the second. Here Juliet's nurse is telling Juliet and her mother exactly how old Juliet is by reminding them she was born the same time as the nurse's daughter, Susan, who has died. In the course of this domestic speech, Shakespeare tells us when and how babies were nursed and weaned and establishes the nurse as a garrulous servant who sees herself as both an important and self-important member of the family.*

Nurse

Even or odd, of all days in the year,
Come Lammas-eve at night shall she be fourteen.
Susan and she--God rest all Christian souls!--
Were of an age: well, Susan is with God;
She was too good for me: but, as I said,
On Lammas-eve at night shall she be fourteen;
That shall she, marry; I remember it well.
'Tis since the earthquake now eleven years;
And she was wean'd,--I never shall forget it,--
Of all the days of the year, upon that day:
For I had then laid wormwood to my dug,
Sitting in the sun under the dove-house wall;
My lord and you were then at Mantua:--
Nay, I do bear a brain:--but, as I said,
When it did taste the wormwood on the nipple

19

Of my dug and felt it bitter, pretty fool,
To see it tetchy and fall out with the dug!
Shake quoth the dove-house: 'twas no need, I trow,
To bid me trudge:
And since that time it is eleven years;
For then she could stand alone; nay, by the rood,
She could have run and waddled all about;
For even the day before, she broke her brow:
And then my husband--God be with his soul!
A' was a merry man--took up the child:
'Yea,' quoth he, 'dost thou fall upon thy face?
Thou wilt fall backward when thou hast more wit;
Wilt thou not, Jule?' and, by my holidame,
The pretty wretch left crying and said 'Ay.'
To see, now, how a jest shall come about!
I warrant, an I should live a thousand years,
I never should forget it: 'Wilt thou not, Jule?' quoth he;
And, pretty fool, it stinted and said 'Ay.'

9.

Romeo and Juliet

Act I Scene 4 Line 53
Mercutio is a lively, volatile, inventive and risk-taking friend of Romeo. He helps persuade Romeo to crash the party where Romeo meets Juliet, and later challenges Tybalt to fight in the street despite the warnings of the Prince against civil brawls. On their way to the Capulet party, Mercutio tells this fanciful story of Queen Mab to impress Romeo and his friends with his wit and invention and to explain Romeo's strange dreams. Mercutio is a role that actors often prefer to play, even above Romeo.

Mercutio

O, then, I see Queen Mab hath been with you.
She is the fairies' midwife, and she comes
In shape no bigger than an agate-stone
On the fore-finger of an alderman,
Drawn with a team of little atomies
Athwart men's noses as they lie asleep;
Her wagon-spokes made of long spiders' legs,
The cover of the wings of grasshoppers,
The traces of the smallest spider's web,
The collars of the moonshine's watery beams,
Her whip of cricket's bone, the lash of film,
Her wagoner a small grey-coated gnat,
Not so big as a round little worm
Prick'd from the lazy finger of a maid;
Her chariot is an empty hazel-nut
Made by the joiner squirrel or old grub,
Time out o' mind the fairies' coachmakers.
And in this state she gallops night by night

Through lovers' brains, and then they dream of love;
O'er courtiers' knees, that dream on court'sies straight,
O'er lawyers' fingers, who straight dream on fees,
O'er ladies ' lips, who straight on kisses dream,
Which oft the angry Mab with blisters plagues,
Because their breaths with sweetmeats tainted are:
Sometime she gallops o'er a courtier's nose,
And then dreams he of smelling out a suit;
And sometime comes she with a tithe-pig's tail
Tickling a parson's nose as a' lies asleep,
Then dreams, he of another benefice:
Sometime she driveth o'er a soldier's neck,
And then dreams he of cutting foreign throats,
Of breaches, ambuscadoes, Spanish blades,
Of healths five-fathom deep; and then anon
Drums in his ear, at which he starts and wakes,
And being thus frighted swears a prayer or two
And sleeps again. This is that very Mab
That plats the manes of horses in the night,
And bakes the elflocks in foul sluttish hairs,
Which once untangled, much misfortune bodes:
This is the hag, when maids lie on their backs,
That presses them and learns them first to bear,
Making them women of good carriage:
This is she. . .
True, I talk of dreams,
Which are the children of an idle brain. . .

10.

Romeo and Juliet

Act I Scene 5 Line 111
Romeo has been in love with Rosaline, but when he sees Juliet all thoughts of Rosaline disappear and he has eyes for no one but Juliet. He asks a servant who she is, but the servant claims not to know. To whom Romeo addresses this speech is unspecified: the servant? Someone else at the party? The audience? Each director will decide along with the actor playing Romeo.

Romeo

O, she doth teach the torches to burn bright!
It seems she hangs upon the cheek of night
Like a rich jewel in an Ethiope's ear;
Beauty too rich for use, for earth too dear!
So shows a snowy dove trooping with crows,
As yonder lady o'er her fellows shows.
The measure done, I'll watch her place of stand,
And, touching hers, make blessed my rude hand.
Did my heart love till now? forswear it, sight!
For I ne'er saw true beauty till this night.

11.

Romeo and Juliet

Act III Scene 2 Line 1
Having secretly married Romeo, Juliet waits for him, eager for their wedding night. In one of Shakespeare's brilliant uses of dramatic irony the dramatist has made sure the audience knows, though she does not, that while she dreams of her husband, Mercutio has been killed by Tybalt, and Romeo has in turn killed Juliet's cousin, Tybalt, setting the tragedy to come.

Juliet

Gallop apace, you fiery-footed steeds,
Towards Phoebus' lodging: such a wagoner
As Phaethon would whip you to the west,
And bring in cloudy night immediately.
Spread thy close curtain, love-performing night,
That runaway's eyes may wink and Romeo
Leap to these arms, untalk'd of and unseen.
Lovers can see to do their amorous rites
By their own beauties; or, if love be blind,
It best agrees with night. Come, civil night,
Thou sober-suited matron, all in black,
And learn me how to lose a winning match,
Play'd for a pair of stainless maidenhoods:
Hood my unmann'd blood, bating in my cheeks,
With thy black mantle; till strange love, grown bold,
Think true love acted simple modesty.
Come, night; come, Romeo; come, thou day in night;
For thou wilt lie upon the wings of night
Whiter than new snow on a raven's back.
Come, gentle night, come, loving, black-brow'd night,

Give me my Romeo; and, when he shall die,
Take him and cut him out in little stars,
And he will make the face of heaven so fine
That all the world will be in love with night
And pay no worship to the garish sun.
O, I have bought the mansion of a love,
But not possess'd it, and, though I am sold,
Not yet enjoy'd: so tedious is this day
As is the night before some festival
To an impatient child that hath new robes
And may not wear them. O, here comes my nurse,
And she brings news; and every tongue that speaks
But Romeo's name speaks heavenly eloquence.
Now, nurse, what news?

12.

Richard II

Act II Scene 1 Line 31
John of Gaunt has watched his nephew Richard II make mistake after mistake while ruling his beautiful country. Richard has established a corrupt regime, giving power and valuable presents to unworthy hangers-on. Gaunt seeks understanding from his brother, the Duke of York. While praising "this royal throne of kings, this sceptered isle", Gaunt, knowing his death is near, dreads what will come next now that England, because of Richard, is "bound in with shame."

John of Gaunt

Methinks I am a prophet new inspired
And thus expiring do foretell of him:
His rash fierce blaze of riot cannot last,
For violent fires soon burn out themselves;
Small showers last long, but sudden storms are short;
He tires betimes that spurs too fast betimes;
With eager feeding food doth choke the feeder:
Light vanity, insatiate cormorant,
Consuming means, soon preys upon itself.
This royal throne of kings, this scepter'd isle,
This earth of majesty, this seat of Mars,
This other Eden, demi-paradise,
This fortress built by Nature for herself
Against infection and the hand of war,
This happy breed of men, this little world,
This precious stone set in the silver sea,
Which serves it in the office of a wall,
Or as a moat defensive to a house,
Against the envy of less happier lands,

This blessed plot, this earth, this realm, this England,
This nurse, this teeming womb of royal kings,
Fear'd by their breed and famous by their birth,
Renowned for their deeds as far from home,
For Christian service and true chivalry,
As is the sepulchre in stubborn Jewry,
Of the world's ransom, blessed Mary's Son,
This land of such dear souls, this dear dear land,
Dear for her reputation through the world,
Is now leased out, I die pronouncing it,
Like to a tenement or pelting farm:
England, bound in with the triumphant sea
Whose rocky shore beats back the envious siege
Of watery Neptune, is now bound in with shame,
With inky blots and rotten parchment bonds:
That England, that was wont to conquer others,
Hath made a shameful conquest of itself.
Ah, would the scandal vanish with my life,
How happy then were my ensuing death!

13.

Richard II

Act III Scene 2 Line 145
*Richard comes home from an ill-considered war in Ireland to hear
from his followers that England under the leadership of John of
Gaunt's son, Henry Bolingbrook, has risen against him. He eagerly
demands reports from various messengers, but all the news is bad.
Richard's power as king is gone forever and his eloquent expression of
grief here and elsewhere in the play have earned him the epithet the
poet king.*

Richard

...Of comfort no man speak:
Let's talk of graves, of worms, and epitaphs;
Make dust our paper and with rainy eyes
Write sorrow on the bosom of the earth,
Let's choose executors and talk of wills:
And yet not so, for what can we bequeath
Save our deposed bodies to the ground?
Our lands, our lives and all are Bolingbroke's,
And nothing can we call our own but death
And that small model of the barren earth
Which serves as paste and cover to our bones.
For God's sake, let us sit upon the ground
And tell sad stories of the death of kings;
How some have been deposed; some slain in war,
Some haunted by the ghosts they have deposed;
Some poison'd by their wives: some sleeping kill'd;
All murder'd: for within the hollow crown
That rounds the mortal temples of a king
Keeps Death his court and there the antic sits,

Scoffing his state and grinning at his pomp,
Allowing him a breath, a little scene,
To monarchize, be fear'd and kill with looks,
Infusing him with self and vain conceit,
As if this flesh which walls about our life,
Were brass impregnable, and humour'd thus
Comes at the last and with a little pin
Bores through his castle wall, and farewell king!
Cover your heads and mock not flesh and blood
With solemn reverence: throw away respect,
Tradition, form and ceremonious duty,
For you have but mistook me all this while:
I live with bread like you, feel want,
Taste grief, need friends: subjected thus,
How can you say to me, I am a king?

14.

A Midsummer Night's Dream

Act II Scene 1 Line 81

Titania, the Queen of the Fairies, meets with Oberon, the Fairy King, in the forest. He calls her proud, accuses her of infidelity, and claims she does not respect him as her lord. In her angry reply, Titania accuses Oberon of causing the miserable weather they are suffering from – endless rain, dying animals, failed crops. These references help date this play to 1594, 95, or 96 as all three of these summers in England were miserably wet and cold.

Titania

These are the forgeries of jealousy:
And never, since the middle summer's spring,
Met we on hill, in dale, forest or mead,
By paved fountain or by rushy brook,
Or in the beached margent of the sea,
To dance our ringlets to the whistling wind,
But with thy brawls thou hast disturb'd our sport.
Therefore the winds, piping to us in vain,
As in revenge, have suck'd up from the sea
Contagious fogs; which falling in the land
Have every pelting river made so proud
That they have overborne their continents:
The ox hath therefore stretch'd his yoke in vain,
The ploughman lost his sweat, and the green corn
Hath rotted ere his youth attain'd a beard;
The fold stands empty in the drowned field,
And crows are fatted with the murrion flock;
The nine men's morris is fill'd up with mud,
And the quaint mazes in the wanton green

For lack of tread are undistinguishable:
The human mortals want their winter here;
No night is now with hymn or carol blest:
Therefore the moon, the governess of floods,
Pale in her anger, washes all the air,
That rheumatic diseases do abound:
And thorough this distemperature we see
The seasons alter: hoary-headed frosts
Far in the fresh lap of the crimson rose,
And on old Hiems' thin and icy crown
An odorous chaplet of sweet summer buds
Is, as in mockery, set: the spring, the summer,
The childing autumn, angry winter, change
Their wonted liveries, and the mazed world,
By their increase, now knows not which is which:
And this same progeny of evils comes
From our debate, from our dissension;
We are their parents and original.

15.

The Merchant of Venice

Act IV Scene 1 Line 183
Portia, disguised as a young male lawyer, has come to the Venetian law courts to try to save the life of Antonio, the merchant of Venice. Antonio has defaulted on a debt he owes to the money lender Shylock and the forfeiture is a pound of his flesh. Admitting that Antonio signed the bond and that Shylock has every right to take his collateral, Portia says that Shylock must then be merciful. "Why?", Shylock asks and Portia replies:

Portia

The quality of mercy is not strain'd,
It droppeth as the gentle rain from heaven
Upon the place beneath: it is twice blest;
It blesseth him that gives and him that takes:
'Tis mightiest in the mightiest: it becomes
The throned monarch better than his crown;
His sceptre shows the force of temporal power,
The attribute to awe and majesty,
Wherein doth sit the dread and fear of kings;
But mercy is above this sceptred sway;
It is enthroned in the hearts of kings,
It is an attribute to God himself;
And earthly power doth then show likest God's
When mercy seasons justice. Therefore, Jew,
Though justice be thy plea, consider this,
That, in the course of justice, none of us
Should see salvation: we do pray for mercy;
And that same prayer doth teach us all to render
The deeds of mercy. I have spoke thus much

To mitigate the justice of thy plea;
Which if thou follow, this strict court of Venice
Must needs give sentence 'gainst the merchant there.

16.

The Merchant of Venice

Act V Scene 1 Line 54

*At the end of **The Merchant of Venice**, the young couple Lorenzo and Jessica have been taking care of Portia's estate while she goes into Venice to the trial of Antonio. The young lovers have come out into the moonlight to await the return of Portia. Lorenzo sets the tone of the ending of this play by looking to the stars and philosophizing with his love.*

Lorenzo

How sweet the moonlight sleeps upon this bank!
Here will we sit and let the sounds of music
Creep in our ears: soft stillness and the night
Become the touches of sweet harmony.
Sit, Jessica. Look how the floor of heaven
Is thick inlaid with patines of bright gold:
There's not the smallest orb which thou behold'st
But in his motion like an angel sings,
Still quiring to the young-eyed cherubins;
Such harmony is in immortal souls;
But whilst this muddy vesture of decay
Doth grossly close it in, we cannot hear it.

17.

King John

Act III Scene 4 Line 93
*Constance was a character much loved by 19th century actresses and **King John** therefore was a favorite work at that time. But the play is not often performed in the 20-21st century. Constance is the mother of the young Arthur, nephew to King John, in line for the throne, popular with John's enemies and therefore a threat to the king. Believing Arthur has died, Constance is grief-struck — so much so she is scolded for her excessive emotion. She turns on the bishops and courtiers who scorn her grief. Because of the depth of feeling in this speech many feel that its writing must have post-dated 1596, the year Shakespeare's own son died at age 11. This would make the speech a rare instance of Shakespeare using his own experience as the direct basis of his writing.*

Constance

Grief fills the room up of my absent child,
Lies in his bed, walks up and down with me,
Puts on his pretty looks, repeats his words,
Remembers me of all his gracious parts,
Stuffs out his vacant garments with his form;
Then, have I reason to be fond of grief?
Fare you well: had you such a loss as I,
I could give better comfort than you do.
I will not keep this form upon my head,
When there is such disorder in my wit.
O Lord! my boy, my Arthur, my fair son!
My life, my joy, my food, my all the world!
My widow-comfort, and my sorrows' cure!

18.

Much Ado About Nothing

Act II Scene 3 Line 7
Benedick and his young friend Claudio serve in the army together. Benedick has had bad luck in love and is shocked and disappointed that his young colleague has carelessly fallen in love. Benedick has several soliloquies in this charming play which are particularly well performed by Kenneth Branagh in his 1993 film.

Benedick

I do much wonder that one man, seeing how much
another man is a fool when he dedicates his
behaviors to love, will, after he hath laughed at
such shallow follies in others, become the argument
of his own scorn by failing in love: and such a man
is Claudio. I have known when there was no music
with him but the drum and the fife; and now had he
rather hear the tabour and the pipe: I have known
when he would have walked ten mile a-foot to see a
good armour; and now will he lie ten nights awake,
carving the fashion of a new doublet. He was wont to
speak plain and to the purpose, like an honest man
and a soldier; and now is he turned orthography; his
words are a very fantastical banquet, just so many
strange dishes. May I be so converted and see with
these eyes? I cannot tell; I think not: I will not
be sworn, but love may transform me to an oyster; but
I'll take my oath on it, till he have made an oyster

of me, he shall never make me such a fool. One woman
is fair, yet I am well; another is wise, yet I am
well; another virtuous, yet I am well; but till all
graces be in one woman, one woman shall not come in
my grace. Rich she shall be, that's certain; wise,
or I'll none; virtuous, or I'll never cheapen her;
fair, or I'll never look on her; mild, or come not
near me; noble, or not I for an angel; of good
discourse, an excellent musician, and her hair shall
be of what colour it please God. Ha! the prince and
Monsieur Love! I will hide me in the arbour.

19.

Much Ado about Nothing

Act II Scene 3 Line 218

Overhearing that Beatrice is in love with him, Benedick finds himself suddenly and unexpectedly in the same boat as the love-sick Claudio. In his 1993 film Branagh makes an interesting interpretive choice at the end of the third and beginning of the fourth line. As punctuated the line would be spoken: "Love me! Why, it must be requited." Branagh says: "Love me? Why?" Then his determination to love her follows with "It must be requited." This choice adds a touching vulnerability to Benedick's character. Is Branagh allowed to do this? Evidently. Punctuation in Shakespeare's day, like spelling, was not fixed: in Hamlet's first soliloquy he describes his flesh as "sullied" or is it "solid"? The choice and thus the interpretation must be made by the actor or director.

Benedick

This can be no trick: the
conference was sadly borne. They have the truth of
this from Hero. They seem to pity the lady: it
seems her affections have their full bent. Love me!
why, it must be requited. I hear how I am censured:
they say I will bear myself proudly, if I perceive
the love come from her; they say too that she will
rather die than give any sign of affection. I did
never think to marry: I must not seem proud: happy
are they that hear their detractions and can put
them to mending. They say the lady is fair; 'tis a
truth, I can bear them witness; and virtuous; 'tis
so, I cannot reprove it; and wise, but for loving
me; by my troth, it is no addition to her wit, nor

no great argument of her folly, for I will be
horribly in love with her. I may chance have some
odd quirks and remnants of wit broken on me,
because I have railed so long against marriage: but
doth not the appetite alter? a man loves the meat
in his youth that he cannot endure in his age.
Shall quips and sentences and these paper bullets of
the brain awe a man from the career of his humour?
No, the world must be peopled. When I said I would
die a bachelor, I did not think I should live till I
were married. Here comes Beatrice. By this day!
she's a fair lady: I do spy some marks of love in her.

20.

Henry IV Part 1

Act V Scene 1 Line 128
Here on the field of the upcoming decisive battle between Prince Hal's army and that of Hotspur, Falstaff asks Prince Hal to help him if he should find himself in trouble. Hal refuses to commit, saying Falstaff owes God a death. In Elizabethan English "death" and "debt" would have both been pronounced the same: "dett". Falstaff's prevarications in this famous speech, and his completely understandable working out an argument that will excuse him from further combat, are an excellent example of the appeal Falstaff has had since he first appeared on the stage. A scutcheon (in the last line) is a painted shield.

Falstaff (referring to his death/debt owed to God)

'Tis not due yet; I would be loath to pay him before
his day. What need I be so forward with him that
calls not on me? Well, 'tis no matter; honour pricks
me on. Yea, but how if honour prick me off when I
come on? how then? Can honour set to a leg? no: or
an arm? no: or take away the grief of a wound? no.
Honour hath no skill in surgery, then? no. What is
honour? a word. What is in that word honour? what
is that honour? air. A trim reckoning! Who hath it?
he that died o' Wednesday. Doth he feel it? no.
Doth he hear it? no. 'Tis insensible, then. Yea,
to the dead. But will it not live with the living?
no. Why? detraction will not suffer it. Therefore
I'll none of it. Honour is a mere scutcheon: and so
ends my catechism.

21.

Henry IV Part 2

Act III Scene 1 Line 4
Alone, trying to sleep, Henry IV works his way to the last line of this speech, one of Shakespeare's most familiar: "Uneasy lies the head that wears a crown." Compare this soliloquy to the first one in this collection – it is a similar meditation on the burden of kingship. Henry IV felt keenly how painful it was to rule when there were questions as to the validity of his right to the throne – questions he acknowledged as justified since he obtained the crown on the death of the rightful king, Richard II, murdered it was believed on Henry's order.

King

How many thousand of my poorest subjects
Are at this hour asleep! O sleep, O gentle sleep,
Nature's soft nurse, how have I frighted thee,
That thou no more wilt weigh my eyelids down
And steep my senses in forgetfulness?
Why rather, sleep, liest thou in smoky cribs,
Upon uneasy pallets stretching thee
And hush'd with buzzing night-flies to thy slumber,
Than in the perfumed chambers of the great,
Under the canopies of costly state,
And lull'd with sound of sweetest melody?
O thou dull god, why liest thou with the vile
In loathsome beds, and leavest the kingly couch
A watch-case or a common 'larum-bell?
Wilt thou upon the high and giddy mast
Seal up the ship-boy's eyes, and rock his brains
In cradle of the rude imperious surge
And in the visitation of the winds,

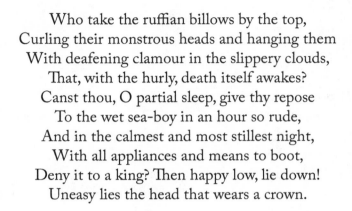

Who take the ruffian billows by the top,
Curling their monstrous heads and hanging them
With deafening clamour in the slippery clouds,
That, with the hurly, death itself awakes?
Canst thou, O partial sleep, give thy repose
To the wet sea-boy in an hour so rude,
And in the calmest and most stillest night,
With all appliances and means to boot,
Deny it to a king? Then happy low, lie down!
Uneasy lies the head that wears a crown.

22.

Henry V

Act 1 Prologue Line 1
*Uniquely, **Henry V** is a play that uses a character named "Chorus"
to introduce each act and to comment on the action of the play. This
appeal to the audience to use their imaginations illustrates the way
a soliloquy involves the direct contact between the speaker and the
audience. **Henry V, Julius Caesar,** and **Hamlet,** all written at
the end of the 1590s, contain more great rhetoric, more memorable
soliloquies and monologues than most of Shakespeare's other plays.*

Chorus

O for a Muse of fire, that would ascend
The brightest heaven of invention,
A kingdom for a stage, princes to act
And monarchs to behold the swelling scene!
Then should the warlike Harry, like himself,
Assume the port of Mars; and at his heels,
Leash'd in like hounds, should famine, sword and fire
Crouch for employment. But pardon, and gentles all,
The flat unraised spirits that have dared
On this unworthy scaffold to bring forth
So great an object: can this cockpit hold
The vasty fields of France? or may we cram
Within this wooden O the very casques
That did affright the air at Agincourt?
O, pardon! since a crooked figure may
Attest in little place a million;
And let us, ciphers to this great accompt,
On your imaginary forces work.
Suppose within the girdle of these walls

Are now confined two mighty monarchies,
Whose high upreared and abutting fronts
The perilous narrow ocean parts asunder:
Piece out our imperfections with your thoughts;
Into a thousand parts divide on man,
And make imaginary puissance;
Think when we talk of horses, that you see them
Printing their proud hoofs i' the receiving earth;
For 'tis your thoughts that now must deck our kings,
Carry them here and there; jumping o'er times,
Turning the accomplishment of many years
Into an hour-glass: for the which supply,
Admit me Chorus to this history;
Who prologue-like your humble patience pray,
Gently to hear, kindly to judge, our play.

23.

Henry V

Act II Prologue
*These next four Choruses from **Henry V** show Shakespeare's skills as
a narrator, and a writer of superb description. He knew of Greek
choruses from his studies in school, but changes the Greek group of a
dozen or so to a single character named Chorus. The choral function is
similar however: to reflect the feelings and thoughts of the community,
to tell us what is happening and how we should respond, and to
connect the players onstage with the audience.*

Chorus

Now all the youth of England are on fire,
And silken dalliance in the wardrobe lies:
Now thrive the armourers, and honour's thought
Reigns solely in the breast of every man:
They sell the pasture now to buy the horse,
Following the mirror of all Christian kings,
With winged heels, as English Mercuries.
For now sits Expectation in the air,
And hides a sword from hilts unto the point
With crowns imperial, crowns and coronets,
Promised to Harry and his followers.
The French, advised by good intelligence
Of this most dreadful preparation,
Shake in their fear and with pale policy
Seek to divert the English purposes.
O England! model to thy inward greatness,
Like little body with a mighty heart,
What mightst thou do, that honour would thee do,
Were all thy children kind and natural!

But see thy fault! France hath in thee found out
A nest of hollow bosoms, which he fills
With treacherous crowns; and three corrupted men,
One, Richard Earl of Cambridge, and the second,
Henry Lord Scroop of Masham, and the third,
Sir Thomas Grey, knight, of Northumberland,
Have, for the gilt of France,--O guilt indeed!
Confirm'd conspiracy with fearful France;
And by their hands this grace of kings must die,
If hell and treason hold their promises,
Ere he take ship for France, and in Southampton.
Linger your patience on; and we'll digest
The abuse of distance; force a play:
The sum is paid; the traitors are agreed;
The king is set from London; and the scene
Is now transported, gentles, to Southampton;
There is the playhouse now, there must you sit:
And thence to France shall we convey you safe,
And bring you back, charming the narrow seas
To give you gentle pass; for, if we may,
We'll not offend one stomach with our play.
But, till the king come forth, and not till then,
Unto Southampton do we shift our scene.

24.

Henry V

Act III Prologue Line 1
Here the Chorus is used to move the action of the play from England to France. The text speaks to the knowledge of English audiences about the sea, the ships that sailed it, and the seamen that manned them.

Chorus

Thus with imagined wing our swift scene flies
In motion of no less celerity
Than that of thought. Suppose that you have seen
The well-appointed king at Hampton pier
Embark his royalty; and his brave fleet
With silken streamers the young Phoebus fanning:
Play with your fancies, and in them behold
Upon the hempen tackle ship-boys climbing;
Hear the shrill whistle which doth order give
To sounds confused; behold the threaden sails,
Borne with the invisible and creeping wind,
Draw the huge bottoms through the furrow'd sea,
Breasting the lofty surge: O, do but think
You stand upon the ravage and behold
A city on the inconstant billows dancing;
For so appears this fleet majestical,
Holding due course to Harfleur. Follow, follow:
Grapple your minds to sternage of this navy,
And leave your England, as dead midnight still,
Guarded with grandsires, babies and old women,
Either past or not arrived to pith and puissance;
For who is he, whose chin is but enrich'd
With one appearing hair, that will not follow

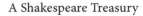

These cull'd and choice-drawn cavaliers to France?
Work, work your thoughts, and therein see a siege;
Behold the ordnance on their carriages,
With fatal mouths gaping on girded Harfleur.
Suppose the ambassador from the French comes back;
Tells Harry that the king doth offer him
Katharine his daughter, and with her, to dowry,
Some petty and unprofitable dukedoms.
The offer likes not: and the nimble gunner
With linstock now the devilish cannon touches,

Alarum, and chambers go off

And down goes all before them. Still be kind,
And eke out our performance with your mind.

25.

Henry V

Act IV Prologue Line 1
*It is quite possible that Shakespeare played the Chorus in performances of **Henry V**. It is argued that he played roles that enabled him to also direct and revise the text, of which the Chorus would be an excellent example. The Epilogue also suggests the it is the writer who is speaking it.*

Chorus

Now entertain conjecture of a time
When creeping murmur and the poring dark
Fills the wide vessel of the universe.
From camp to camp through the foul womb of night
The hum of either army stilly sounds,
That the fixed sentinels almost receive
The secret whispers of each other's watch:
Fire answers fire, and through their paly flames
Each battle sees the other's umber'd face;
Steed threatens steed, in high and boastful neighs
Piercing the night's dull ear, and from the tents
The armourers, accomplishing the knights,
With busy hammers closing rivets up,
Give dreadful note of preparation:
The country cocks do crow, the clocks do toll,
And the third hour of drowsy morning name.
Proud of their numbers and secure in soul,
The confident and over-lusty French
Do the low-rated English play at dice;
And chide the cripple tardy-gaited night
Who, like a foul and ugly witch, doth limp

So tediously away. The poor condemned English,
Like sacrifices, by their watchful fires
Sit patiently and inly ruminate
The morning's danger, and their gesture sad
Investing lank-lean; cheeks and war-worn coats
Presenteth them unto the gazing moon
So many horrid ghosts. O now, who will behold
The royal captain of this ruin'd band
Walking from watch to watch, from tent to tent,
Let him cry 'Praise and glory on his head!'
For forth he goes and visits all his host.
Bids them good morrow with a modest smile
And calls them brothers, friends and countrymen.
Upon his royal face there is no note
How dread an army hath enrounded him;
Nor doth he dedicate one jot of colour
Unto the weary and all-watched night,
But freshly looks and over-bears attaint
With cheerful semblance and sweet majesty;
That every wretch, pining and pale before,
Beholding him, plucks comfort from his looks:
A largess universal like the sun
His liberal eye doth give to every one,
Thawing cold fear, that mean and gentle all,
Behold, as may unworthiness define,
A little touch of Harry in the night. . .

26.

Henry V

Act IV Scene 1 Line 135
*Henry has gone in disguise from campfire to campfire to learn the
feelings of his soldiers. They know he is taking them into a battle in
which they will be facing an enormous, rich, well-equipped, rested
French army while they are a small, weak, wasted force at best.
Williams is one of the soldiers gathered around the fire, and sometimes
is played as one of the boys who are later slaughtered by the cruel
French. Here he speaks honestly to the man he does not know is the
king, thus piling responsibility onto Henry.*

Williams

But if the cause be not good, the king himself hath
a heavy reckoning to make, when all those legs and
arms and heads, chopped off in battle, shall join
together at the latter day and cry all 'We died at
such a place;' some swearing, some crying for a
surgeon, some upon their wives left poor behind
them, some upon the debts they owe, some upon their
children rawly left. I am afeard there are few die
well that die in a battle; for how can they
charitably dispose of anything, when blood is their
argument? Now, if these men do not die well, it
will be a black matter for the king that led them to
it; whom to disobey were against all proportion of
subjection.

27.

Henry V

Compare this soliloquy to the speeches of Henry IV and Henry VI above – all meditations on the difficulties of being king. Again, it must have pleased Elizabeth I and James I to hear their plight expressed with such depth of understanding. Shakespeare's company (first the Lord Chamberlain's Men; then the King's Men) were booked to play at court more than any other companies of the time.

Act IV Scene 1 Line 235

Henry

Upon the king! let us our lives, our souls,
Our debts, our careful wives,
Our children and our sins lay on the king!
We must bear all. O hard condition,
Twin-born with greatness, subject to the breath
Of every fool, whose sense no more can feel
But his own wringing! What infinite heart's-ease
Must kings neglect, that private men enjoy!
And what have kings, that privates have not too,
Save ceremony, save general ceremony?
And what art thou, thou idle ceremony?
What kind of god art thou, that suffer'st more
Of mortal griefs than do thy worshippers?
What are thy rents? what are thy comings in?
O ceremony, show me but thy worth!
What is thy soul of adoration?
Art thou aught else but place, degree and form,
Creating awe and fear in other men?
Wherein thou art less happy being fear'd

Than they in fearing.
What drink'st thou oft, instead of homage sweet,
But poison'd flattery? O, be sick, great greatness,
And bid thy ceremony give thee cure!
Think'st thou the fiery fever will go out
With titles blown from adulation?
Will it give place to flexure and low bending?
Canst thou, when thou command'st the beggar's knee,
Command the health of it? No, thou proud dream,
That play'st so subtly with a king's repose;
I am a king that find thee, and I know
'Tis not the balm, the sceptre and the ball,
The sword, the mace, the crown imperial,
The intertissued robe of gold and pearl,
The farced title running 'fore the king,
The throne he sits on, nor the tide of pomp
That beats upon the high shore of this world,
No, not all these, thrice-gorgeous ceremony,
Not all these, laid in bed majestical,
Can sleep so soundly as the wretched slave,
Who with a body fill'd and vacant mind
Gets him to rest, cramm'd with distressful bread;
Never sees horrid night, the child of hell,
But, like a lackey, from the rise to set
Sweats in the eye of Phoebus and all night
Sleeps in Elysium; next day after dawn,
Doth rise and help Hyperion to his horse,
And follows so the ever-running year,
With profitable labour, to his grave:
And, but for ceremony, such a wretch,
Winding up days with toil and nights with sleep,
Had the fore-hand and vantage of a king.

28.

Henry V

Having prepared for battle and prayed for God's help, Henry overhears Westmorland wishing they had even a few more soldiers to take into battle against the French. This speech is referred to as the St. Crispin's Day speech and from it comes Henry's immortal claim that all who fight with him are a "band of brothers." Winston Churchill is said to have encouraged Laurence Olivier to film this play in order to raise the morale of the British during the dark times of World War II.

Act IV Scene 3 Line 19

Henry

What's he that wishes so?
My cousin Westmoreland? No, my fair cousin:
If we are mark'd to die, we are enow
To do our country loss; and if to live,
The fewer men, the greater share of honour.
God's will! I pray thee, wish not one man more.
By Jove, I am not covetous for gold,
Nor care I who doth feed upon my cost;
It yearns me not if men my garments wear;
Such outward things dwell not in my desires:
But if it be a sin to covet honour,
I am the most offending soul alive.
No, faith, my coz, wish not a man from England:
God's peace! I would not lose so great an honour
As one man more, methinks, would share from me
For the best hope I have. O, do not wish one more!
Rather proclaim it, Westmoreland, through my host,
That he which hath no stomach to this fight,

Let him depart; his passport shall be made
And crowns for convoy put into his purse:
We would not die in that man's company
That fears his fellowship to die with us.
This day is called the feast of Crispian:
He that outlives this day, and comes safe home,
Will stand a tip-toe when the day is named,
And rouse him at the name of Crispian.
He that shall live this day, and see old age,
Will yearly on the vigil feast his neighbours,
And say 'To-morrow is Saint Crispian.'
Then will he strip his sleeve and show his scars.
And say 'These wounds I had on Crispin's day.'
Old men forget: yet all shall be forgot,
But he'll remember with advantages
What feats he did that day: then shall our names.
Familiar in his mouth as household words
Harry the king, Bedford and Exeter,
Warwick and Talbot, Salisbury and Gloucester,
Be in their flowing cups freshly remember'd.
This story shall the good man teach his son;
And Crispin Crispian shall ne'er go by,
From this day to the ending of the world,
But we in it shall be remember'd;
We few, we happy few, we band of brothers;
For he to-day that sheds his blood with me
Shall be my brother; be he ne'er so vile,
This day shall gentle his condition:
And gentlemen in England now a-bed
Shall think themselves accursed they were not here,
And hold their manhoods cheap whiles any speaks
That fought with us upon Saint Crispin's day.

29.

Julius Caesar

Act II Scene 1 Line 233

*Shakespeare wrote **Julius Caesar** close to the same time as **Henry V,
As You Like It** and **Hamlet,** about 1599-1600. His gift for making
history come to life is evident here. In the middle of the night a group of
conspirators come to the house of the Roman hero, Brutus, and persuade
him that killing Julius Caesar is the only way to prevent his becoming
a tyrant and turning the Roman republic into a dictatorship. As the
men leave, Brutus's wife Portia appears to plead with her husband to
inform her of what is happening. Some scholars claim Shakespeare did
not write about happy marriages, but this speech seems to reveal an
exceptionally close relationship between Portia and Brutus.*

Portia

You've ungently, Brutus,
Stole from my bed: and yesternight, at supper,
You suddenly arose, and walk'd about,
Musing and sighing, with your arms across,
And when I ask'd you what the matter was,
You stared upon me with ungentle looks;
I urged you further; then you scratch'd your head,
And too impatiently stamp'd with your foot;
Yet I insisted, yet you answer'd not,
But, with an angry wafture of your hand,
Gave sign for me to leave you: so I did;
Fearing to strengthen that impatience
Which seem'd too much enkindled, and withal
Hoping it was but an effect of humour,
Which sometime hath his hour with every man.
It will not let you eat, nor talk, nor sleep,

And could it work so much upon your shape
As it hath much prevail'd on your condition,
I should not know you, Brutus. Dear my lord,
Make me acquainted with your cause of grief. . .
Is Brutus sick? and is it physical
To walk unbraced and suck up the humours
Of the dank morning? What, is Brutus sick,
And will he steal out of his wholesome bed,
To dare the vile contagion of the night
And tempt the rheumy and unpurged air
To add unto his sickness? No, my Brutus;
You have some sick offence within your mind,
Which, by the right and virtue of my place,
I ought to know of: and, upon my knees,
I charm you, by my once-commended beauty,
By all your vows of love and that great vow
Which did incorporate and make us one,
That you unfold to me, yourself, your half,
Why you are heavy, and what men to-night
Have had to resort to you: for here have been
Some six or seven, who did hide their faces
Even from darkness. . .
Within the bond of marriage, tell me, Brutus,
Is it excepted I should know no secrets
That appertain to you? Am I yourself
But, as it were, in sort or limitation,
To keep with you at meals, comfort your bed,
And talk to you sometimes? Dwell I but in the suburbs
Of your good pleasure? If it be no more,
Portia is Brutus' harlot, not his wife. . .
I grant I am a woman; but withal
A woman that Lord Brutus took to wife:
I grant I am a woman; but withal
A woman well-reputed, Cato's daughter.

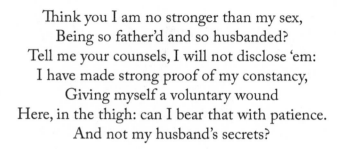

Think you I am no stronger than my sex,
Being so father'd and so husbanded?
Tell me your counsels, I will not disclose 'em:
I have made strong proof of my constancy,
Giving myself a voluntary wound
Here, in the thigh: can I bear that with patience.
And not my husband's secrets?

30.

Julius Caesar

Act III Scene 2 Line 12
A riotous crowd gathers and calls for the death of the men who have just killed Julius Caesar. Brutus faces them and with this passionate but closely reasoned oration barely manages to calm them.

Brutus

Romans, countrymen, and lovers! hear me for my
cause, and be silent, that you may hear: believe me
for mine honour, and have respect to mine honour, that
you may believe: censure me in your wisdom, and
awake your senses, that you may the better judge.
If there be any in this assembly, any dear friend of
Caesar's, to him I say, that Brutus' love to Caesar
was no less than his. If then that friend demand
why Brutus rose against Caesar, this is my answer:
--Not that I loved Caesar less, but that I loved
Rome more. Had you rather Caesar were living and
die all slaves, than that Caesar were dead, to live
all free men? As Caesar loved me, I weep for him;
as he was fortunate, I rejoice at it; as he was
valiant, I honour him: but, as he was ambitious, I
slew him. There is tears for his love; joy for his
fortune; honour for his valour; and death for his
ambition. Who is here so base that would be a
bondman? If any, speak; for him have I offended.
Who is here so rude that would not be a Roman? If
any, speak; for him have I offended. Who is here so
vile that will not love his country? If any, speak;
for him have I offended. I pause for a reply.

31.

Julius Caesar

Act III Scene 2 Line 77
Brutus makes a tactical but idealistic error in leaving the Forum and allowing Mark Antony to speak to the rioters alone. Antony takes the arguments of Brutus and cleverly reverses them, reinvigorating the fear and anger felt by the crowd at the death of Caesar. Shakespeare is a master of crowd psychology as this speech and its further development in the play demonstrate.

Antony

Friends, Romans, countrymen, lend me your ears;
I come to bury Caesar, not to praise him.
The evil that men do lives after them;
The good is oft interred with their bones;
So let it be with Caesar. The noble Brutus
Hath told you Caesar was ambitious:
If it were so, it was a grievous fault,
And grievously hath Caesar answer'd it.
Here, under leave of Brutus and the rest--
For Brutus is an honourable man;
So are they all, all honourable men--
Come I to speak in Caesar's funeral.
He was my friend, faithful and just to me:
But Brutus says he was ambitious;
And Brutus is an honourable man.
He hath brought many captives home to Rome
Whose ransoms did the general coffers fill:
Did this in Caesar seem ambitious?
When that the poor have cried, Caesar hath wept:
Ambition should be made of sterner stuff:

Yet Brutus says he was ambitious;
And Brutus is an honourable man.
You all did see that on the Lupercal
I thrice presented him a kingly crown,
Which he did thrice refuse: was this ambition?
Yet Brutus says he was ambitious;
And, sure, he is an honourable man.
I speak not to disprove what Brutus spoke,
But here I am to speak what I do know.
You all did love him once, not without cause:
What cause withholds you then, to mourn for him?
O judgment! thou art fled to brutish beasts,
And men have lost their reason. Bear with me;
My heart is in the coffin there with Caesar,
And I must pause till it come back to me.

32.

As You Like It

Act II Scene 7 Line 139

Shakespeare was not the first nor the only Elizabethan writer to explore the idea that "All the world's a stage" or to divide a man's life into different ages. But Shakespeare's development of the image has proven memorable. The setting is the Forest of Arden. Jaques is one of a number of aristocrats exiled by a powerful duke. Jaques speaks to the exiles who have just welcomed to their midst an old man and his companion, the young Orlando. As they exit to find a place of rest for Adam, the old man, the Duke observes

Thou seest we are not all alone unhappy.
This wide and universal theater
Presents more woeful pageants than this scene
Wherein we play in.

And Jacques replies:

Jacques

All the world's a stage,
And all the men and women merely players:
They have their exits and their entrances;
And one man in his time plays many parts,
His acts being seven ages. At first the infant,
Mewling and puking in the nurse's arms.
And then the whining school-boy, with his satchel
And shining morning face, creeping like snail
Unwillingly to school. And then the lover,
Sighing like furnace, with a woeful ballad
Made to his mistress' eyebrow. Then a soldier,
Full of strange oaths and bearded like the pard,
Jealous in honour, sudden and quick in quarrel,

Seeking the bubble reputation
Even in the cannon's mouth. And then the justice,
In fair round belly with good capon lined,
With eyes severe and beard of formal cut,
Full of wise saws and modern instances;
And so he plays his part. The sixth age shifts
Into the lean and slipper'd pantaloon,
With spectacles on nose and pouch on side,
His youthful hose, well saved, a world too wide
For his shrunk shank; and his big manly voice,
Turning again toward childish treble, pipes
And whistles in his sound. Last scene of all,
That ends this strange eventful history,
Is second childishness and mere oblivion,
Sans teeth, sans eyes, sans taste, sans everything.

33.

Twelfth Night

Act II Scene 2 Line 12
Viola is dressed as a young man, Cesario, and has found work in the household of the Duke Orsino. Orsino has commanded Cesario to woo on his behalf his lovely neighbor Olivia. She has no use for Orsino, but finds herself miraculously attracted to the page, Cesario. Disappointed by his/her lack of success in promoting the Duke's affections, yet relieved because she (Viola/Cesario) is herself falling in love with Orsino, Cesario leaves Olivia's house only to be followed by Olivia's steward Malvolio who brings Cesario a ring Olivia claims was left her by the page. This is a ploy to get Cesario to come back to continue his master's suit so that Olivia can see him again. The progressive discoveries and realizations in this soliloquy make it a popular choice for young actresses auditioning for Shakespearean plays – so popular that directors sometimes ask it not be done in auditions – they've seen it all too often.

Viola

I left no ring with her: what means this lady?
Fortune forbid my outside have not charm'd her!
She made good view of me; indeed, so much,
That sure methought her eyes had lost her tongue,
For she did speak in starts distractedly.
She loves me, sure; the cunning of her passion
Invites me in this churlish messenger.
None of my lord's ring! why, he sent her none.
I am the man: if it be so, as 'tis,
Poor lady, she were better love a dream.
Disguise, I see, thou art a wickedness,
Wherein the pregnant enemy does much.

How easy is it for the proper-false
In women's waxen hearts to set their forms!
Alas, our frailty is the cause, not we!
For such as we are made of, such we be.
How will this fadge? my master loves her dearly;
And I, poor monster, fond as much on him;
And she, mistaken, seems to dote on me.
What will become of this? As I am man,
My state is desperate for my master's love;
As I am woman,--now alas the day!--
What thriftless sighs shall poor Olivia breathe!
O time! thou must untangle this, not I;
It is too hard a knot for me to untie!

PART 4 GREAT TRAGEDIES AND PROBLEM PLAYS 1600-1610

34.

Hamlet

Act I Scene 2 Line 129
Hamlet has returned to Elsinore, his home in Denmark, for the celebration of his mother's marriage to his uncle Claudius. He is tormented by the speed of this marriage, following within weeks of his father's death. This soliloquy is the first of eight monologues revealing the depth of feeling and the complex psychology of Shakespeare's best-known character.

Hamlet

O, that this too too solid flesh would melt
Thaw and resolve itself into a dew!
Or that the Everlasting had not fix'd
His canon 'gainst self-slaughter! O God! God!
How weary, stale, flat and unprofitable,
Seem to me all the uses of this world!
Fie on't! ah fie! 'tis an unweeded garden,
That grows to seed; things rank and gross in nature
Possess it merely. That it should come to this!
But two months dead: nay, not so much, not two:
So excellent a king; that was, to this,
Hyperion to a satyr; so loving to my mother
That he might not beteem the winds of heaven
Visit her face too roughly. Heaven and earth!
Must I remember? why, she would hang on him,
As if increase of appetite had grown
By what it fed on: and yet, within a month--

Let me not think on't--Frailty, thy name is woman!--
A little month, or ere those shoes were old
With which she follow'd my poor father's body,
Like Niobe, all tears:--why she, even she--
O, God! a beast, that wants discourse of reason,
Would have mourn'd longer--married with my uncle,
My father's brother, but no more like my father
Than I to Hercules: within a month:
Ere yet the salt of most unrighteous tears
Had left the flushing in her galled eyes,
She married. O, most wicked speed, to post
With such dexterity to incestuous sheets!
It is not nor it cannot come to good:
But break, my heart; for I must hold my tongue.

35.

Hamlet

Act II Scene 2 Line 561

A company of touring actors arrives in Elsinore. Hamlet asks for a sample of their work and finds himself moved by the Player King's deep feeling as he acts the part of Priam, Hecuba's husband, in a play about the Trojan War. Here the themes of seeming and being, of acting and reality, and particularly of self-doubt are explored as Hamlet determines to trap the king into a revelation of his guilt. Hamlet speaks as the players have exited.

Hamlet

Now I am alone.
O, what a rogue and peasant slave am I!
Is it not monstrous that this player here,
But in a fiction, in a dream of passion,
Could force his soul so to his own conceit
That from her working all his visage wann'd,
Tears in his eyes, distraction in's aspect,
A broken voice, and his whole function suiting
With forms to his conceit? and all for nothing!
For Hecuba!
What's Hecuba to him, or he to Hecuba,
That he should weep for her? What would he do,
Had he the motive and the cue for passion
That I have? He would drown the stage with tears
And cleave the general ear with horrid speech,
Make mad the guilty and appal the free,
Confound the ignorant, and amaze indeed
The very faculties of eyes and ears. Yet I,
A dull and muddy-mettled rascal, peak,

Like John-a-dreams, unpregnant of my cause,
And can say nothing; no, not for a king,
Upon whose property and most dear life
A damn'd defeat was made. Am I a coward?
Who calls me villain? breaks my pate across?
Plucks off my beard, and blows it in my face?
Tweaks me by the nose? gives me the lie i' the throat,
As deep as to the lungs? who does me this?
Ha!
'Swounds, I should take it: for it cannot be
But I am pigeon-liver'd and lack gall
To make oppression bitter, or ere this
I should have fatted all the region kites
With this slave's offal: bloody, bawdy villain!
Remorseless, treacherous, lecherous, kindless villain!
O, vengeance!
Why, what an ass am I! This is most brave,
That I, the son of a dear father murder'd,
Prompted to my revenge by heaven and hell,
Must, like a whore, unpack my heart with words,
And fall a-cursing, like a very drab,
A scullion!
Fie upon't! foh! About, my brain! I have heard
That guilty creatures sitting at a play
Have by the very cunning of the scene
Been struck so to the soul that presently
They have proclaim'd their malefactions;
For murder, though it have no tongue, will speak
With most miraculous organ. I'll have these players
Play something like the murder of my father
Before mine uncle: I'll observe his looks;
I'll tent him to the quick: if he but blench,
I know my course. The spirit that I have seen
May be the devil: and the devil hath power

To assume a pleasing shape; yea, and perhaps
Out of my weakness and my melancholy,
As he is very potent with such spirits,
Abuses me to damn me: I'll have grounds
More relative than this: the play 's the thing
Wherein I'll catch the conscience of the king.

36.

Hamlet

Act III Scene 1 Line 56

This soliloquy, the most famous of Hamlet's monologues, reveals his longing for the courage to commit suicide. Step by step he discovers why it is difficult for humans, he among them, to take this dire action.

Hamlet

To be, or not to be, that is the question,
Whether 'tis nobler in the mind to suffer
The slings and arrows of outrageous fortune,
Or to take arms against a sea of troubles,
And by opposing end them? To die: to sleep;
No more; and by a sleep to say we end
The heart-ache and the thousand natural shocks
That flesh is heir to, 'tis a consummation
Devoutly to be wish'd. To die, to sleep;
To sleep: perchance to dream: ay, there's the rub;
For in that sleep of death what dreams may come
When we have shuffled off this mortal coil,
Must give us pause: there's the respect
That makes calamity of so long life;
For who would bear the whips and scorns of time,
The oppressor's wrong, the proud man's contumely,
The pangs of despised love, the law's delay,
The insolence of office and the spurns
That patient merit of the unworthy takes,
When he himself might his quietus make
With a bare bodkin? who would fardels bear,
To grunt and sweat under a weary life,
But that the dread of something after death,

The undiscover'd country from whose bourn
No traveller returns, puzzles the will
And makes us rather bear those ills we have
Than fly to others that we know not of?
Thus conscience does make cowards of us all;
And thus the native hue of resolution
Is sicklied o'er with the pale cast of thought,
And enterprises of great pith and moment
With this regard their currents turn awry,
And lose the name of action

37.

Hamlet

Act III Scene 2 Line 1

Having decided to put on the play, Hamlet knows it is imperative that the performance be perfectly acted. This speech is given to the players as they are readying themselves for performance. Written in prose as befits the workmanlike situation, the speech is filled with nervous energy and pre-show jitters. Shakespeare may have seen medieval performances in Coventry when he was young where the villain, Herod, would over-act with audience-pleasing bombast which explains "out Herods Herod."

Hamlet

Speak the speech, I pray you, as I pronounced it to
you, trippingly on the tongue: but if you mouth it,
as many of your players do, I had as lief the
town-crier spoke my lines. Nor do not saw the air
too much with your hand, thus, but use all gently;
for in the very torrent, tempest, and, as I may say,
the whirlwind of passion, you must acquire and beget
a temperance that may give it smoothness. O, it
offends me to the soul to hear a robustious
periwig-pated fellow tear a passion to tatters, to
very rags, to split the ears of the groundlings, who
for the most part are capable of nothing but
inexplicable dumbshows and noise: I would have such
a fellow whipped for o'erdoing Termagant; it
out-herods Herod: pray you, avoid it. . .
Be not too tame neither, but let your own discretion
be your tutor: suit the action to the word, the
word to the action; with this special o'erstep not

the modesty of nature: for anything so overdone is
from the purpose of playing, whose end, both at the
first and now, was and is, to hold, as 'twere, the
mirror up to nature; to show virtue her own feature,
scorn her own image, and the very age and body of
the time his form and pressure. Now this overdone,
or come tardy off, though it make the unskilful
laugh, cannot but make the judicious grieve; the
censure of the which one must in your allowance
o'erweigh a whole theatre of others. O, there be
players that I have seen play, and heard others
praise, and that highly, not to speak it profanely,
that, neither having the accent of Christians nor
the gait of Christian, pagan, nor man, have so
strutted and bellowed that I have thought some of
nature's journeymen had made men and not made them
well, they imitated humanity so abominably. . .
And let those that play
your clowns speak no more than is set down for them;
for there be of them that will themselves laugh, to
set on some quantity of barren spectators to laugh
too; though, in the mean time, some necessary
question of the play be then to be considered:
that's villanous, and shows a most pitiful ambition
in the fool that uses it. Go, make you ready.

38.

Hamlet

Act IV Scene 4 Line 32
On his way to England, sent by Claudius, Hamlet meets with a Captain of the Norwegian army leading a company to a fight over worthless piece of land in Poland. This encounter forces Hamlet to recognize his inadequacies and to recommit to avenging his father's murder.

Hamlet

How all occasions do inform against me,
And spur my dull revenge! What is a man,
If his chief good and market of his time
Be but to sleep and feed? a beast, no more.
Sure, he that made us with such large discourse,
Looking before and after, gave us not
That capability and god-like reason
To fust in us unused. Now, whether it be
Bestial oblivion, or some craven scruple
Of thinking too precisely on the event,
A thought which, quarter'd, hath but one part wisdom
And ever three parts coward, I do not know
Why yet I live to say 'This thing's to do;'
Sith I have cause and will and strength and means
To do't. Examples gross as earth exhort me:
Witness this army of such mass and charge
Led by a delicate and tender prince,
Whose spirit with divine ambition puff'd
Makes mouths at the invisible event,
Exposing what is mortal and unsure
To all that fortune, death and danger dare,

Even for an egg-shell. Rightly to be great
Is not to stir without great argument,
But greatly to find quarrel in a straw
When honour's at the stake. How stand I then,
That have a father kill'd, a mother stain'd,
Excitements of my reason and my blood,
And let all sleep? while, to my shame, I see
The imminent death of twenty thousand men,
That, for a fantasy and trick of fame,
Go to their graves like beds, fight for a plot
Whereon the numbers cannot try the cause,
Which is not tomb enough and continent
To hide the slain? O, from this time forth,
My thoughts be bloody, or be nothing worth!

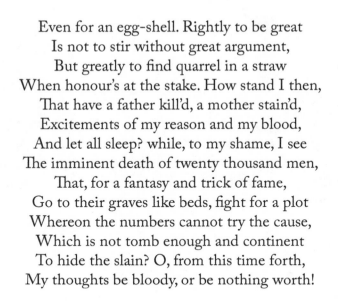

39.

Hamlet

Act IV Scene 7 Line 164
*The violent death of her father at Hamlet's hand, Hamlet's treatment
of her, and Laertes' absence in France, have driven Ophelia to madness
and death. The queen has to tell Claudius and Laertes (just returned
from France) the manner of Ophelia's death.*

Queen

There is a willow grows aslant a brook,
That shows his hoar leaves in the glassy stream;
There with fantastic garlands did she come
Of crow-flowers, nettles, daisies, and long purples
That liberal shepherds give a grosser name,
But our cold maids do dead men's fingers call them:
There, on the pendent boughs her coronet weeds
Clambering to hang, an envious sliver broke;
When down her weedy trophies and herself
Fell in the weeping brook. Her clothes spread wide;
And, mermaid-like, awhile they bore her up:
Which time she chanted snatches of old tunes;
As one incapable of her own distress,
Or like a creature native and indued
Unto that element: but long it could not be
Till that her garments, heavy with their drink,
Pull'd the poor wretch from her melodious lay
To muddy death.

40.

Troilus and Cressida

Act III Scene 3 Line 144
Ulysses, thought to be the wisest and wiliest of the Greek invaders of Troy, has been asked to persuade the great warrior Achilles to stop pouting in his tent, forget his petty grievances, and come out to fight. Ulysses explains that Achilles's reputation will continue to rust as long as he keeps himself out of sight. Shakespeare knew well humans are judged for what they are doing in the present moment. What anyone once did is always and inevitably soon forgotten.

Ulysses

Time hath, my lord, a wallet at his back,
Wherein he puts alms for oblivion,
A great-sized monster of ingratitudes:
Those scraps are good deeds past; which are devour'd
As fast as they are made, forgot as soon
As done: perseverance, dear my lord,
Keeps honour bright: to have done is to hang
Quite out of fashion, like a rusty mail
In monumental mockery. Take the instant way;
For honour travels in a strait so narrow,
Where one but goes abreast: keep then the path;
For emulation hath a thousand sons
That one by one pursue: if you give way,
Or hedge aside from the direct forthright,
Like to an enter'd tide, they all rush by
And leave you hindmost;
Or like a gallant horse fall'n in first rank,
Lie there for pavement to the abject rear,
O'er-run and trampled on: then what they do in present,

Though less than yours in past, must o'ertop yours;
For time is like a fashionable host
That slightly shakes his parting guest by the hand,
And with his arms outstretch'd, as he would fly,
Grasps in the comer: welcome ever smiles,
And farewell goes out sighing. O, let not
virtue seek
Remuneration for the thing it was;
For beauty, wit,
High birth, vigour of bone, desert in service,
Love, friendship, charity, are subjects all
To envious and calumniating time.
One touch of nature makes the whole world kin,
That all with one consent praise new-born gawds,
Though they are made and moulded of things past,
And give to dust that is a little gilt
More laud than gilt o'er-dusted.
The present eye praises the present object.
Then marvel not, thou great and complete man,
That all the Greeks begin to worship Ajax;
Since things in motion sooner catch the eye
Than what not stirs. The cry went once on thee,
And still it might, and yet it may again,
If thou wouldst not entomb thyself alive
And case thy reputation in thy tent;
Whose glorious deeds, but in these fields of late,
Made emulous missions 'mongst the gods themselves
And drave great Mars to faction.

41.

King Lear

Act I Scene 2 Line 1
Edmund is the bastard son of Gloucester, one of King Lear's close friends. His illegitimate status rankles and embitters him and he uses it to excuse his betrayal of his brother Edgar. Not a loving God but fickle Nature is the entity he worships.

Edmund

Thou, nature, art my goddess; to thy law
My services are bound. Wherefore should I
Stand in the plague of custom, and permit
The curiosity of nations to deprive me,
For that I am some twelve or fourteen moon-shines
Lag of a brother? Why bastard? wherefore base?
When my dimensions are as well compact,
My mind as generous, and my shape as true,
As honest madam's issue? Why brand they us
With base? with baseness? bastardy? base, base?
Who, in the lusty stealth of nature, take
More composition and fierce quality
Than doth, within a dull, stale, tired bed,
Go to the creating a whole tribe of fops,
Got 'tween asleep and wake? Well, then,
Legitimate Edgar, I must have your land:
Our father's love is to the bastard Edmund
As to the legitimate: fine word,--legitimate!
Well, my legitimate, if this letter speed,
And my invention thrive, Edmund the base
Shall top the legitimate. I grow; I prosper:
Now, gods, stand up for bastards!

42.

King Lear

Act II Scene 2 Line 10
Kent is a loyal subject to his beloved King Lear. Having helped Lear,
he will find himself punished soon by the king's evil daughter Regan.
Kent meets with Oswald, steward to Lear's second daughter, Goneril,
as each join the family and servants at Gloucester's home. There is no
love lost between Kent and Oswald and when Oswald treats him
casually as a servant Kent lets loose one of Shakespeare's most brilliant
tirades (using the same figure, systrophy, we observed in Petruchio's
speech in the first section of this book).

Kent

[Fellow, I know thee for]
A knave; a rascal; an eater of broken meats; a
base, proud, shallow, beggarly, three-suited,
hundred-pound, filthy, worsted-stocking knave; a
lily-livered, action-taking knave, a whoreson,
glass-gazing, super-serviceable finical rogue;
one-trunk-inheriting slave; one that wouldst be a
bawd, in way of good service, and art nothing but
the composition of a knave, beggar, coward, pandar,
and the son and heir of a mongrel bitch: one whom I
will beat into clamorous whining, if thou deniest
the least syllable of thy addition. . .
What a brazen-faced varlet art thou, to deny thou
knowest me! Is it two days ago since I tripped up
thy heels, and beat thee before the king? Draw, you
rogue: for, though it be night, yet the moon
shines; I'll make a sop o' the moonshine of you:
draw, you whoreson cullionly barber-monger, draw.

43.

Othello

Act 4 Scene 3 Line 69
The lovely and innocent Desdemona is shocked to learn it is thought most people are unfaithful to their spouses. She finds it impossible to believe and asks her more experienced lady in waiting---and friend-- Emilia if she would ever do such a thing or knows women who do. Emilia, concerned that Desdemona's innocence will harm her in the end, answers with a surprisingly tart and contemporary reply.

Emilia

Yes, a dozen.
But I do think it is their husbands' faults
If wives do fall: say that they slack their duties,
And pour our treasures into foreign laps,
Or else break out in peevish jealousies,
Throwing restraint upon us; or say they strike us,
Or scant our former having in despite;
Why, we have galls, and though we have some grace,
Yet have we some revenge. Let husbands know
Their wives have sense like them: they see and smell
And have their palates both for sweet and sour,
As husbands have. What is it that they do
When they change us for others? Is it sport?
I think it is: and doth affection breed it?
I think it doth: is't frailty that thus errs?
It is so too: and have not we affections,
Desires for sport, and frailty, as men have?
Then let them use us well: else let them know,
The ills we do, their ills instruct us so.

44.

Othello

Act V Scene 2 Line 1
*Convinced his wife has been unfaithful to him (the cause of his need for
vengeance), Othello creeps into her dark and silent bedroom knowing
he must kill her. He will punish her and thus prevent her from ever
tempting and "betraying more men". Shakespeare's powerful use
of double irony – the audience knows what Othello does not, that
Desdemona is innocent, and knows, as Desdemona does not, that he is
there to kill her-- makes this scene almost unbearable to watch.*

Othello

It is the cause, it is the cause, my soul,--
Let me not name it to you, you chaste stars!--
It is the cause. Yet I'll not shed her blood;
Nor scar that whiter skin of hers than snow,
And smooth as monumental alabaster.
Yet she must die, else she'll betray more men.
Put out the light, and then put out the light:
If I quench thee, thou flaming minister,
I can again thy former light restore,
Should I repent me: but once put out thy light,
Thou cunning'st pattern of excelling nature,
I know not where is that Promethean heat
That can thy light relume. When I have pluck'd the rose,
I cannot give it vital growth again.
It must needs wither: I'll smell it on the tree.

Kissing her

Ah balmy breath, that dost almost persuade

Justice to break her sword! One more, one more.
Be thus when thou art dead, and I will kill thee,
And love thee after. One more, and this the last:
So sweet was ne'er so fatal. I must weep,
But they are cruel tears: this sorrow's heavenly;
It strikes where it doth love. She wakes.

45.

Measure for Measure

Act III Scene 1 Line 117

Claudio is a young man imprisoned and condemned to death for the sin of fornication. His sister, Isabella, can save his life if she will sleep with Angelo, the recently appointed ruler of Vienna, a man chosen for his hitherto stringent morality. When Isabella pleads for her brother's compassion, and begs that he not force her — she, a novice about to become a nun — to commit such an act, Claudio at first agrees. But the fear of death comes upon him and he pleads in turn for her understanding.

Claudio

Ay, but to die, and go we know not where;
To lie in cold obstruction and to rot;
This sensible warm motion to become
A kneaded clod; and the delighted spirit
To bathe in fiery floods, or to reside
In thrilling region of thick-ribbed ice;
To be imprison'd in the viewless winds,
And blown with restless violence round about
The pendent world; or to be worse than worst
Of those that lawless and incertain thought
Imagine howling: 'tis too horrible!
The weariest and most loathed worldly life
That age, ache, penury and imprisonment
Can lay on nature is a paradise
To what we fear of death.

46.

Macbeth

Act III Scene 2 Line 46

Macbeth has lied to two potential murderers, telling them Banquo is responsible for their impoverished state. Macbeth implies he will reward them for killing Banquo. Corrupting these men and arranging the murder of Banquo are evils so profound that Macbeth can't even describe this "deed of dreadful note" to his wife when she asks him "What's to be done?"

Macbeth

Be innocent of the knowledge, dearest chuck,
Till thou applaud the deed. Come, seeling night,
Scarf up the tender eye of pitiful day;
And with thy bloody and invisible hand
Cancel and tear to pieces that great bond
Which keeps me pale! Light thickens; and the crow
Makes wing to the rooky wood:
Good things of day begin to droop and drowse;
While night's black agents to their preys do rouse.
Thou marvell'st at my words: but hold thee still;
Things bad begun make strong themselves by ill.
So, prithee, go with me.

47.

Macbeth

Act V Scene 5 Line 20
Macduff and Malcolm's forces are near. Macbeth enters, filled with a desperate energy. As his soldiers leave, a cry of women is heard. Macbeth asks, "What is that noise" and is told by Seyton, his attendant, that "The queen, my lord, is dead." Macbeth's answer reveals the depths to which his relentlessly evil choices have lead him.

Macbeth

She should have died hereafter;
There would have been a time for such a word.
To-morrow, and to-morrow, and to-morrow,
Creeps in this petty pace from day to day
To the last syllable of recorded time,
And all our yesterdays have lighted fools
The way to dusty death. Out, out, brief candle!
Life's but a walking shadow, a poor player
That struts and frets his hour upon the stage
And then is heard no more: it is a tale
Told by an idiot, full of sound and fury,
Signifying nothing.

48.

Antony and Cleopatra

Act V Scene 2 Line 75
Mark Antony is dead. Cleopatra knows if she surrenders to Octavius Caesar she will be taken to Rome as a captive. As she awaits Caesar for their final interview, Cleopatra speaks to Caesar's follower, Dolabella. She would have them know—and Dolabella acknowledge—how pathetic all the Roman soldiers are compared to Mark Antony. She will not die until the world knows his quality.

Cleopatra

I dream'd there was an Emperor Antony:
O, such another sleep, that I might see
But such another man!. . .
His face was as the heavens; and therein stuck
A sun and moon, which kept their course,
and lighted
The little O, the earth. . .
His legs bestrid the ocean: his rear'd arm
Crested the world: his voice was propertied
As all the tuned spheres, and that to friends;
But when he meant to quail and shake the orb,
He was as rattling thunder. For his bounty,
There was no winter in't; an autumn 'twas
That grew the more by reaping: his delights
Were dolphin-like; they show'd his back above
The element they lived in: in his livery
Walk'd crowns and crownets; realms and islands were
As plates dropp'd from his pocket. . .
Think you there was, or might be, such a man
As this I dream'd of?

[No?]
You lie, up to the hearing of the gods.
But, if there be, or ever were, one such,
It's past the size of dreaming: nature wants stuff
To vie strange forms with fancy; yet, to imagine
An Antony, were nature's piece 'gainst fancy,
Condemning shadows quite.

PART 5 THE LATE ROMANCES 1607-1611

49.

The Winter's Tale

Act IV Scene 4 Line 103
*Perdita is a shepherd girl asked by her father to be, for the first time, the hostess of an annual sheep-shearing party. One of her chores is to hand out flowers to welcome newcomers. She discovers much later she is the daughter of King Leontes, and the man she loves is the son of the local king – one of the middle-aged men to whom she has shyly given flowers. The late Romances, the last plays (except for **Henry VIII**) Shakespeare wrote are filled with love, with images of nature, with forgiveness and with compassion. Those who enjoy creating Shakespeare gardens use this monologue of Perdita's as one of the sources to identify the flowers Shakespeare knew and loved.*

Perdita

Here's flowers for you;
Hot lavender, mints, savoury, marjoram;
The marigold, that goes to bed wi' the sun
And with him rises weeping: these are flowers
Of middle summer, and I think they are given
To men of middle age. You're very welcome...
I would I had some flowers o' the spring that might
Become your time of day; and yours, and yours,
That wear upon your virgin branches yet
Your maidenheads growing: O Proserpina,
For the flowers now, that frighted thou let'st fall
From Dis's waggon! daffodils,
That come before the swallow dares, and take
The winds of March with beauty; violets dim,

But sweeter than the lids of Juno's eyes
Or Cytherea's breath; pale primroses . . .
bold oxlips and
The crown imperial; lilies of all kinds,
The flower-de-luce being one!

50.

The Tempest

Act III Scene 3 Line148
Caliban is the half-wild son of the witch Sycorax. Prospero has held him as a slave since his (Prospero's) arrival on the island decades ago. Caliban offers his services to Stephano and Trinculo, recently come to the island in a shipwreck, in hopes they will help him get revenge on Prospero. This monologue spoken to Stephano and Trinculo is surprising and challenges the actor and director to justify such sensitive imagery coming from the mouth of a character who seems in many ways a stone-age monster.

Caliban

Be not afeard; the isle is full of noises,
Sounds and sweet airs, that give delight and hurt not.
Sometimes a thousand twangling instruments
Will hum about mine ears, and sometime voices
That, if I then had waked after long sleep,
Will make me sleep again: and then, in dreaming,
The clouds methought would open and show riches
Ready to drop upon me that, when I waked,
I cried to dream again.

51.

The Tempest

Act IV Scene 1 Line 148
Prospero has staged an engagement celebration for his daughter Miranda and future son-in-law Ferdinand. This party takes the form of a Jacobean masque, i.e. a feast and a lush, musical entertainment with appearances of the gods and other classical allusions. Elaborate scenery and costumes are important elements. Prospero brings the celebration to a close with this unforgettable comparison of life to the theatrical event he has created.

Prospero

Our revels now are ended. These our actors,
As I foretold you, were all spirits and
Are melted into air, into thin air:
And, like the baseless fabric of this vision,
The cloud-capp'd towers, the gorgeous palaces,
The solemn temples, the great globe itself,
Yea all which it inherit, shall dissolve
And, like this insubstantial pageant faded,
Leave not a rack behind. We are such stuff
As dreams are made on, and our little life
Is rounded with a sleep.

52.

The Tempest

Act V Scene 1 Line 132
Left alone after he sends his spirit Ariel to gather the others, Prospero readies himself to leave his island, saying farewell to the creatures he has come to know and the extraordinary life he has led there. As this was the next-to-last work Shakespeare wrote (the last he wrote on his own, without a collaborator) some readers can't but feel that with this speech Shakespeare says his farewell to his art: to his writing, to his acting, and to his long life in the theatre.

Prospero

Ye elves of hills, brooks, standing lakes and groves,
And ye that on the sands with printless foot
Do chase the ebbing Neptune and do fly him
When he comes back; you demi-puppets that
By moonshine do the green sour ringlets make,
Whereof the ewe not bites, and you whose pastime
Is to make midnight mushrooms, that rejoice
To hear the solemn curfew; by whose aid,
Weak masters though ye be, I have bedimm'd
The noontide sun, call'd forth the mutinous winds,
And 'twixt the green sea and the azured vault
Set roaring war: to the dread rattling thunder
Have I given fire and rifted Jove's stout oak
With his own bolt; the strong-based promontory
Have I made shake and by the spurs pluck'd up
The pine and cedar: graves at my command
Have waked their sleepers, oped, and let 'em forth
By my so potent art. But this rough magic
I here abjure, and, when I have required

Some heavenly music, which even now I do,
To work mine end upon their senses that
This airy charm is for, I'll break my staff,
Bury it certain fathoms in the earth,
And deeper than did ever plummet sound
I'll drown my book.